INVERTEBRATES

ANIMALS IN DISGUISE

Lynn Stone

The Rourke Corporation, Inc.
Vero Beach, Florida 32964

PHOTO CREDITS
© Peter James: cover, title page, pages 7, 15, 18; © Lynn M. Stone: pages 4, 8, 10, 12, 13, 17, 21 and small cover photo

EDITORIAL SERVICES:
Penworthy Learning Systems

Library of Congress Cataloging-in-Publication Data

Stone, Lynn M.
    Invertebrates / Lynn M. Stone.
        p. cm. — (Animals in disguise)
    Includes index
    Summary: Describes how various invertebrates use ways to disguise themselves and fool other animals, including camouflage and other tricks with color and shape.
    ISBN 0-86593-489-4
    1. Invertebrates—Juvenile literature. 2. Camouflage (Biology) —Juvenile literature.
    [1. Invertebrates. 2. Camouflage (Biology)] I. Title II. Series. Stone, Lynn M. Animals in disguise.
    QL362.4.S76 1998
    592.147'2—dc21
                                                                    98–6324
                                                                    CIP
                                                                    AC

Printed in the USA

TABLE OF CONTENTS

INVERTEBRATES

"Invertebrate" (in VER tuh BRAYT) is a big word for a group of mostly very little animals. Some of the animals you know best are invertebrates. Among them are insects, octopuses, spiders, clams, crabs, and worms.

Invertebrates don't have bones inside their bodies. And because they are small, invertebrates are often **prey** (PRAY), or food, for larger animals. Many invertebrates, however, keep themselves from being eaten by using **disguise** (dis GYZ).

This stick insect is disguised as a long, thin twig.

STAYING ALIVE

A disguise changes how an animal looks to other animals. Many invertebrates can look like something they're not. That way they can avoid trouble—and live another day.

Every animal tries to **survive** (sur VYV), or stay alive, as long as it can. An animal wants to eat, but not be eaten.

Disguise is often a good way for an invertebrate to find food. It's an even better way not to become food!

This crab spider's disguise as part of the flower helped it make a meal of a fly.

INVERTEBRATES IN DISGUISE

For many invertebrates, every day is like Halloween. These animals are masters of disguise. They almost never appear as what they really are.

What happens to a spider if it doesn't look like a spider? For one thing, a spider-eating **predator** (PRED uh tur), or hunter, probably won't find it. For another, the spider in disguise can fool its prey. If a prey animal doesn't recognize a spider, it won't try to avoid the spider.

The green lynx is a master of camouflage among green plants.

CRYPTIC COLORS

Invertebrates have many ways to disguise themselves. One of the best is **cryptic** (KRIP tik) colors. Those are colors that blend with the animal's habitat, or home.

Cryptic colors allow an invertebrate to disguise, or **camouflage** (KAM uh FLAHJ), itself as part of its habitat. Some invertebrates can change their cryptic colors. When their habitat changes, their bodies change colors to match.

This mantis in Costa Rica looks like a pair of leaves.

The ghost crab's cryptic shell is a match for the crab's beach home.

The polyphemus moth of North America wears giant eyespots on its back wings to fool predators.

CAMOUFLAGE

Certain kinds of shrimp, crabs, squid, octopus, and spiders are among the invertebrates that change colors. In some animals, this quick turn of disguise takes just seconds.

Some invertebrates can almost "disappear" without the help of cryptic colors. Sound impossible? Certain shrimp, for example, have see-through bodies, almost like clear glass. Their surroundings show through them! Instead of seeing a shrimp, a predator sees only the object behind the shrimp.

This anemone shrimp, clear as glass, hides among the long, arms of a sea anemone.

SHAPES

Some invertebrates build their disguise around the color and shape of objects near them. Stick insects and their relatives may look like twigs, pieces of straw, or leaves. One **species** (SPEE sheez), or kind, looks like an orchid! When insects visit this "flower," it bites.

The treehopper looks like a thorn. The dead-leaf butterfly looks like an old, brown leaf. Several kinds of katydids and bush crickets look like leaves, too. One spider species looks like bird droppings.

The treehopper's disguise makes it look more like a thorn than an insect.

MIMICS

Some invertebrates **mimic** (MIM ik), or copy, the shapes and colors of other animals. By mimicking, an animal gains some benefit. A caterpillar of Central America has markings that make it look like a snake instead of a harmless insect.

Some moths and butterflies mimic bees, but the moths and butterflies have no stingers. The viceroy butterfly mimics the bitter-tasting monarch butterfly.

This katydid looks like the lichens growing on this tree in Ecuador.

BORROWED DISGUISES

Certain invertebrates borrow disguises from their habitat or from other animals. Hermit crabs hide out in the shells of snails. Their disguise fails only when the crabs move about.

In the wormlike stage of its life, the caddisfly hides on stream bottoms. But it doesn't hide in mud. It covers itself with stones!

The masking crab hangs bits of sponge and seaweed from its body. The decorator shell sticks other shells to its own.

A caddisfly nymph, hidden in a disguise of stones, spends winter in an Illinois stream.

EYESPOTS

Large animal eyes can be scary to other animals. Many invertebrates have tiny eyes. But with make-believe eyes, called eyespots, these invertebrates can sometimes scare away predators. Eyespots also disguise the whereabouts of an animal's real head and eyes.

Many moths and butterflies wear eyespots. Their fake eyes are on their wings. Certain grasshoppers and caterpillars have eyespots, too.

Glossary

camouflage (KAM uh FLAHJ) — the ability of an animal to use color, actions, and shape to blend into its surroundings

cryptic (KRIP tik) — that which helps hide, such as the colors of an animal that help it hide in its surroundings

disguise (dis GYZ) — a way of changing an animal's appearance

mimic (MIM ik) — to copy the behavior or appearance of another; an animal that copies another's behavior or appearance

invertebrate (in VER tuh BRAYT) — a simple, boneless animal, such as a worm, snail, starfish, or slug

predator (PRED uh tur) — an animal that hunts other animals for food

prey (PRAY) — an animal that is hunted by other animals

species (SPEE sheez) — within a group of closely related plants or animals, one certain kind, such as a *ghost crab*

survive (sur VYV) — to stay alive

INDEX

FURTHER READING:

Find out more about Animals in Disguise with these helpful books:

• Carter, Kyle. *Animals That Survive.* Rourke, 1995
• Greenway, Theresa. *Jungle.* Knopf, 1994
• Mound, Laurence. *Insect.* Knopf, 1990
• Stone, Lynn. *Animals of the Rain Forest.* Rourke, 1994